Smile Through It All

By

Pamela Porter

Smile Through It All

Smile Through It All

By

Pamela Porter

Alopecia Awareness & Domestic Violence Awareness

©

Sunny's Light Enterprises, LLC, 2020 Publishing Co.

www.sunnyslightllc.com

United States Copyright Office

ISBN 978-1-7329989-4-0

Printed in the United States of America 2020

Smile Through It All

About the Author

In writing this book, I've discovered so many things about myself. These discoveries have helped me to come to the realization that I have to continue learning to love myself in the way I want to be loved by others. They have also helped me to have learned that I cannot keep looking for the kind of love that I desire in others before having learned to love myself.

There's one love in particular though that I will always desire despite my condition and that is my Big Granny's love. Big Granny's love filled a space in my heart that no one else has ever been able to fill. I know that she is in heaven above and I have to continuously embrace her love in the spiritual. I imagine that she would not be happy about some of the ways I've chosen to live my life, but I was and sometimes still am a lost soul trying to find my way. It is my hope that Big Granny understands.

I've tried many different ways to achieve happiness, but the best way for me is to just be me and let God take over. Ultimately, he knows the desires of our hearts and becoming an Author was one of those desires. In life we all will make mistakes, but if we fail big enough, we will have learned our true measure of resilience and as a result, we will make better decisions.

Love shouldn't hurt. Instead, love should bring about a positive feeling and be something that is good for you. One day I pray to have a relationship with someone that sees me as a gift from God. I pray and look forward to being in that person's life to help and to love them as they will help and love me. I have so much love in my heart that is just begging to pour into the right person but in the meantime, I will continue focusing on my purpose, aspirations, and becoming the person God called me to be.

I tell people all the time that my past is what has made me the woman I am today. God has helped me to practice the golden rule; to do unto others as I would have them do unto me. I love life, want to experience life, and I'm no longer afraid of life. I keep reminding myself that everyone doesn't think or act like me, we're all different. I understand that sometimes people just need to see that doing it another way can still get you the same results and that is why I chose to tell my story. I am not telling my story to hurt anyone. I am telling my story just to help those who I can help and to connect with those who may have walked or are walking in my shoes.

I am a survivor of domestic violence, I live with Alopecia daily which means that I also deal with the stares that come with being bald, and I live with the fear of ending up with Alzheimer's just as my father did. Although I deal with negative aspects of having Alopecia, I have received a lot of praise for being brave enough to be able to show my beautiful bald head. It took years to get to this point in my life and now not only am I able to show my head, I am able to share just a portion of my journey in hopes that it will educate, inspire, and empower you.

I see a great future ahead for me. God has gotten me this far in life and I'm sure he's going to be there every step of the way for the rest of my life and so I refuse to frown. I am choosing over and over again to SMILE THROUGH IT ALL.

Smile Through It All

Smile Through It All

Chronology

Dedication

To my Big Granny in Heaven,

Thank you for showing me unconditional love for the first 12 years of my life. Yes, I hated it when God called you home, but I was young and didn't understand why you had to leave me. I miss you so much.

Love,

Your Grandbaby

Smile Through It All

Acknowledgements

I would like to thank my mom for giving me life at such a young age. I would also like to thank my kids for being such great kids. Of course, there were challenges but they were great kids for the most part.

Being a single mom is hard and accepting that you have to cut the apron strings completely can be rough but it has to be done in order for them to grow. I thank God for allowing me to be around to see you both grow into such caring gentlemen.

I would like to thank the staff at Juan (Poppy) Abbott Center aka Eastlawn, Community Center and the staff of the Boys and Girls Club of Topeka, if it weren't for these two centers, I am not sure what it could have been for me or who I would have turned out to be.

I want to thank everyone that has been a part of my upbringing and those that were a shoulder to cry on or a listening ear when I needed one.

Last but not least, I would like to thank you the reader for choosing my book to read and as I always say, remember to SMILE THROUGH IT ALL. God bless you.

Smile Through It All

June 4, 1984

The day my innocence was no longer. I had liked him for years. This day, we were about to do something we shouldn't have been doing at our age. The trouble was, he was showing me attention, and when you're yearning for love, any attention will do. See, it goes back to June 26, 1982, when my Big

Granny left this earth to be with the Lord.

That's when my world changed forever. I

started looking for love in all the wrong

places. I used to spend a lot of time with my

Big Granny, and now I didn't have her to talk

to or do things with. When this cute boy who

I'd liked for years showed that he liked me

too, I was all smiles. After a year, I guess

sexing me wasn't good enough for him. He

started seeing other girls and all I could do

was watch him move on with them. That was

when a part of me found out what revenge

was all about. It was like, "Okay, two can play

this game." So, I started showing other guys I

liked just how much I really liked them. I

made sure one day that he knew it, too. You
see, one of the guys I was interested in was
visiting him, and so I called to talk to his
friend for a moment. Next, he knew, his
friend made up an excuse to leave his house.
He didn't know his friend was coming to see
me, but I guess he noticed his friend didn't
leave the neighborhood. Soon after his friend
returned, I had a phone call during which he
only said, "Hope you had fun," and hung up.
All I did was smile, said, "He cares, he cares,"
and went to bed. My high school years were
hard. I was shy and not really popular – or if I
was popular, I didn't know it. I tried going out
for sports to just keep from having to go

home and be alone. My sister had friends she could hang with and talk to, but I couldn't say the same. Our mom had wanted us to come right home after school and stay there. We couldn't have company inside since she wasn't there to see who we were letting in. I started going to the Boy's and Girl's club just to have something to do. All it did was help me get closer to guys I liked but was too shy to say something to. Playing them in basketball, or hanging out in the weight room, or teen room playing games, gave me something to talk about. During my high school days, I used to really wish my mom had more time to spend with me like my Big Granny did, but she

worked nights. It was mainly cleaning on
Saturdays, along with getting clothes ready for
Sunday. Sundays were mainly church all day
and getting ready for the school week. I don't
remember us really talking about girl stuff or
what I wanted to do when I grew up. I just
really felt alone. I guess that's why I turned to
guys more because they were showing me
attention, not thinking it was because I was
giving them what they wanted. But in a way, I
guess they were giving me what I wanted, too.
I guess you can say sex was my drug of
choice. I didn't do like some kids my age,
drinking or smoking (cigs or weed), or
popping pills. I chose to use sex to numb my

need for love. During those times, I didn't have to think of anything but how I was feeling. Later, reality set in that those boys didn't really love me, but got what they wanted out of me: sex. I started realizing that I was the other girl, that they had a girlfriend and just never really said anything to me. They would have me come over at night after their girlfriends had already left, I guess. My biggest highlight of high school was my senior year. I was in the talent show at school. I made my own routine and that was the first time my mom got to see me dance. I also ran for Miss Fashionetta 1987. I was glad and shocked I ran, but I had a good time. I came in third, even though there were only four of us

running. My downfall of high school was not

having a boyfriend and getting stood up for

the prom. I almost had a boyfriend, but he got

his last girlfriend pregnant. His mom told us

all we could be was friends since he now had

responsibilities.

May 24, 1987

This was the day I almost didn't see. I got into a car accident four days prior, which almost ruined things, but to walk across that stage and accept my diploma was a great day in my life. I really wished my Big Granny could have been there to see me, but I know she was smiling down on me that day. I had enrolled at Washburn University for the fall and thought I had a job lined up through my mom's work. Since I was only 17, they couldn't give it to me or hold it for my birthday in a month and a half. I thought of joining the Army, but after passing the test, I got scared of leaving home and decided not to go forward with it. My next move was to go on to college. Unfortunately, I quit after the first semester. After that, I got up the courage to ask my dad if I could come and visit him so I could meet my siblings. Of course, at the time, I only thought I had four of them. For years, I thought I was the big sister of both my parents' kids, but that year I found out I had more siblings than I thought. There were eight through my dad (one older sister, one older brother, three younger sisters, and three

younger brothers) and I was very happy to

meet them. They accepted me as if we grew

up around each other all our lives. I love them

all.

June 6, 1988

My life changed forever. I was now only 18 and dating a 24-year-old, so my mom told me to get back on the pill. Well, in Kansas – or maybe anywhere – once you've been on the pill, you have to take a pregnancy test before getting back on it. This ended up being the day I was told I was going to be a mom. It's also the day I thought I was about to lose my boyfriend. It definitely wasn't his baby because we hadn't had sex yet. I thought my

mom was going to kick me out of the house
for getting pregnant. No one in my family
knew I'd been having sex for the last four
years. Everyone thought I was still a virgin,
and I was very ashamed to tell anyone that I
was pregnant. The shocking part was, I was
already four months along and knew nothing
about becoming a mom, but something in me
took to the idea and ran with it. It was like I
grew up overnight. I changed my room
around and tore all the posters off my wall. I
started babysitting until I couldn't do it
anymore to pay for anything I needed for my
baby. I was very happy that my boyfriend
stayed with me until my son was nine months

old. My family wasn't upset with me either. I

had a lot of support; they even threw me a

baby shower.

November 19, 1988

4:10 AM, God granted me a little boy, who I almost died having. You see, I went into labor on the 18th, but didn't know it. I went to my regular OBGYN appointment and was told my blood pressure was up, so I should lay on my left side and they would check back on me. Since my blood pressure wouldn't go down, they sent me straight to the hospital and I found out I was in labor as well as having preeclampsia, aka toxemia. The

doctor's office had called the hospital while I
was on my way (two blocks) to it. There, a
nurse was already waiting on me, and since I
had done my homework and pre-registered,
they wheeled me right up to prepare for my
baby to arrive a week early. He was due on
Thanksgiving, but I guess he couldn't wait
that long. I was shocked at how many people
came to the hospital to see me during my
labor. I had a great labor coach who told me
to leave that hollering for your pushing,
because I was going to need that energy. The
thought makes me laugh out loud. After 12
hours of labor, my son arrived. Three days
later, he got to go home, but I had to stay in

the hospital since my blood pressure was still

too high. I begged the doctor to let me go

home. I had never been alone away from

home before, so it was a little scary to be in

the hospital without my family. My boyfriend,

though, was so nice to come up every night

after work and sit with me since he lived

down the street from the hospital. My mom

had to take care of my son until I was

released, and my boyfriend remained in our

lives until he went back to his hometown. It

took me a long time to get over him, but I

had to move on for myself and my son. I

started school and a job to try to take care of

us, and keeping busy helped prevent me from

turning to a guy for my lonely needs.

July 12, 1991

My own Independence Day. My 21st birthday

present to myself was my own place. I was

out of school and had a fulltime job now. It

was weird at first and very lonely, but I had

my son and we did a lot of things to keep

from getting bored. He was very hyper, and I

didn't know if that was normal or something

was wrong with him, because he just wouldn't

sit still for too long. Nothing really kept his

attention for a long period of time. So, I had

him tested and was told he had ADHD, aka

Attention Deficit Hyperactivity Disorder.

They put him on meds, and boy what a

difference I saw in him. Some people didn't

think I should have given him the meds, but

they weren't the ones living with him. I was,

and I needed a break from yelling for him to

sit down all the time. I had to do what was

best for me and him, but didn't know it was

going to test my parenting skills. Of course,

by then, he was only three and I didn't know a

lot about how to take care of a boy, let alone a

boy with ADHD. I fell into depression

because not only was I trying to take care of

my son alone, I yearned for companionship. I
kind of fell back into my old teenage ways,
except now that I had a kid, I couldn't always
just have men over since I didn't want my son
around a lot of men. One day, I was feeling
really low and had some really bad thoughts.
To silence them and rid myself of the lonely
feeling, I had decided that day was the last day
I wanted to be on this earth. I got a butcher
knife and a bottle of aspirins and sat at the
table thinking of which one to use to take my
life. I was really missing my Big Granny and
wishing she was there to help me and talk to
me. I decided to call my mom and told her
what I was planning to do. All she told me to

do was pray about it. I was like, "You're not coming to stop me?" It made me even more upset that she was going to just let me kill myself. At that moment, I heard my son move in the bed. I guess that was God's way of saying, "Not now." When I was laying in the hospital after my son's birth, I had asked Him to help me to get my son to at least his 18th birthday. It wasn't time for me to leave this earth yet.

June 7, 1992

I met my husband this day, though I didn't
know that's what he would become. I saw him
at Hillcrest Community Center during the
Juneteenth celebration. My son and I were
leaving the event when I drove past him; it
was like slow motion when our eyes met.
Later that night, I was talking to my best
friend. She mentioned a guy she thought
would be great for me. I was like, Yeah, okay.

Me, being the lonely person, I was, though, said, "Who is that?" She gave me his number, and I called. After talking a little, he asked if he could come by. It took some begging, but I gave in and said okay. In my apartment, you had to buzz people into the building. Since I didn't really know this guy, I went down to the door instead of letting him in. When I saw him, I thought, He looks familiar. Not only was he the guy from the Juneteenth Celebration, I also knew of him from high school. We talked some down at the door and intuition told me it was okay to let him up. My son was asleep upstairs anyway, so I felt I needed to get back before he woke up. From that day, we talked and saw each other daily. I

couldn't wait to get off of work, pick up my

son, and head over to see him. I think I lost

around 10 pounds that month because I

wasn't really eating much. I'd eat breakfast

and lunch at work, but I really wasn't eating

dinner. I made sure my son ate, but I was too

excited when I knew I was about to go see

him. Well, within two months or so, he was

moving in with us, since we were always

together. Might as well make it easier on my

gas tank. We hit it off really well, talks were

great, turned out I knew a lot of his family

and didn't know it. He was a great cook, he

helped keep my place clean, and he got along

great with my son. After a little, we moved out of the apartment and into a house since we now had a dog and she was tearing the place up. Time went by, and some things were changing. Of course, since I didn't want to be alone again, I ignored them for the most part. That is, until one day he said something that just made me pack up everything and move. After a month of being apart, we saw that we really loved each other and wanted to make this relationship work. We moved back in together, and after about two or three months, we got engaged. We decided to get married on my Big Granny's birthday since it fell on a Saturday that year. That meant we had six months to prepare for the wedding.

Well, God must have been happy with our

commitment to each other, because in May of

that year, he gave us an early wedding present:

it turned out I was three months pregnant. I

had just gotten my wedding outfit, and now I

was worried about if it was going to fit. By the

time the wedding came around, I was five

months pregnant and still looking great. I was

very happy that my outfit still fit. Something

wasn't sitting right, though. I had started

wondering if God was seeing something I was

turning a blind eye to. The night before our

wedding, there was a bad storm. The day of, I

put his wedding band on the wrong hand.

That night, a whole new chapter in my life started. We came home to a yard full of his family and friends when I really just wanted to spend the night doing what newlyweds do. Even though I was five months pregnant, that didn't stop me from being able to please my husband. I was really seeing that his family was more important than I was. It was something I'd kinda noticed before, since the night our baby was conceived – aka Valentine's day – he went out with his nephews' rather than staying home with me. That weekend was nice, though. We went out to eat and got some movies to watch since we didn't have money for a honeymoon. In the end, we picked up my son from his grandma's

and shot off fireworks in the front yard.

July 9, 1994

This was the first day my vows were tested.

One week after getting married, I found

myself in the hospital because of my husband.

He was dealing with some medical issues, and

we didn't know what exactly was wrong at the

time. I don't know what I said to push him

over the edge to start cussing me out and

tossing the wedding gifts at me. All I could do

was try and get my son and myself out of

there. Three times he tossed glass from the set

we were given at me. The last time, it broke

and shattered on my right hand. My son and I ran to the car and he came running out with a towel to wrap my hand in. After I took the towel from him, I took off for my mom's house, where my mom watched my son and my sister ran me to the hospital because my hand wouldn't stop bleeding. I had to get six stitches in my right hand and a stress test to check on my baby. Once I told the doctor and cops what happened, they went looking for my husband. I knew they wouldn't find him though. I was sure he'd left the house. The rest of that weekend, I stayed at my mom's place. The sad part was, my birthday was three days later. He had pawned his wedding ring to his mom so he could buy me a present, but

I'm sure he bought more for himself with that

money than he did for me. I ended up going

home, and things seemed okay for the most

part. We were back on track.

October 28, 1994

5:01 AM, my 2nd son was born, and luckily this time, labor went smoother than it did with my first son. The sad part is, I was at the hospital alone the day after he was born. You would think my husband or family would have been there, but it was like no one cared. Everyone was doing their own thang. I decided to get my tubes tied after I had my son. I drove myself to the hospital for the procedure and I just felt so alone to be going into surgery with no support. Even my mom didn't come to the hospital. I guess she

thought my husband was going to be with me.

Sometimes I just wondered what I did to

deserve what I was going through. For the

next three years, I went through more than I

ever thought I would. God was really on my

side. I helped my husband deal with his

medical situation while also dealing with him

doing drugs and drinking beer all the time. I

would go to work just so we could have

money, but also so I could be out of the

house. It was getting to me that I felt like the

man of the house. My husband was always

cussing me out, wondering where I had been

when he already knew where I had been. He

was doing more and more drugs, and I was falling into depression. I felt like my boys were all I was living for. We moved to a bigger place, which I thought would be a good start for us to build a better life. I got a better job and another car. I even decided to go back to school. My husband ruined those things, though, too. I had to quit my job because he kept calling there, and I had to leave school because he kept accusing me of cheating on him. I got a night job, and one night, I skipped out on going and went right to the casino. I wanted to know what it was like to mess up all the money and not care that I had bills to pay. I wanted to be my

husband and see what it was like to act like I
didn't have a family to care for. Only thing is,
I came home and told him what I did, and
next I knew, I was being called a liar. All
because I was supposed to go to work and I
chose to go to the casino. It didn't matter all I
had been through with him; the abuse just
became something as a result of what was in
his head that told him I was doing stuff I
wasn't. I put up with not knowing when he
was going to be mad at me for whatever
reason. He had abused me in every way
possible. If I didn't want to have sex, too bad,
we were having it anyway. I didn't hang with
friends because he would think I had some

man waiting over there for me to see. All I did
was go to work and go home. I hit a low point
in my life when I was working at Kmart. I
chose to steal some cassette tapes because I
never had money for myself; it always went to
bills, daycare, or my husband. I was fired and
banned from coming back into the building.
That was when I had figured I had to do
better in my life. I decided to go to my
husband's nephew's house to rewrite my
résumé with his computer. My husband
decided to tell me if I went over there to not
come back. I was like, Hold up. I'm trying to
get a better job to bring in more money, and
you're forbidding me to go redo my resume?

So that was the day I packed what I could for both of my sons and walked out the door. My car had been so messed up by him and his sister from their drug and beer runs, I had to get on a city bus. I went to his nephew's place to redo my résumé, and since my older son's school wasn't that far, I stayed there until school was out. Afterward, we went to my mom's house. I ended up talking to my husband about ending our marriage, but I guess he must have thought I was playing. By now, I only came to the house on the weekends and went back to my mom's place during the week. I became what I called a weekend wife. That stopped once I got my own place, went back to school, and got

another job. My life became my boys and my

success. I didn't have time to be trying to go

see him.

April 9, 1998

I had been looking forward to this morning for six months, but while I was getting ready for court and the kids ready for daycare and school, I didn't know I was about to have an unexpected visitor. We were getting ready to head out the door when I heard a knock. I peeked out the peephole, and who do I see on the other end of the door but my soon to be ex-husband. You see, that was the day we were getting our divorce, but I wasn't sure if he knew that. I asked him what was he doing there and he said he needed me to take him home. I asked how he got to my place, and he claimed he was in the area. Hmmm. At close to 8 AM? Yeah, okay. Since I didn't have time to argue with him and needed to drop off the boys, I said, "Fine, let's go." I was going to drop him off before I took our son to the daycare, but he requested I do it the other way around. I was like, Why? I have an appointment after I drop our son off. Again, he insisted I drop off our son first. So, I did as he asked. I started to turn off the car and take the keys and my purse, but he said, "No, leave the keys. That way you don't try nothing

funny." I was looking like, what would I try?
I'm trying to get to the courthouse on time.
Again, I did as he said anyway, but I made
sure I took my purse. I took our son to his
daycare room and gave him a kiss, then I went
to check him in at the front desk. While I was
up there, I asked if I could use their phone so
I could call the cops. I had no clue what was
about to happen to me if I got in that car
alone with my husband. I had to explain to
them he was out in my car and I was to be
headed to the courthouse to get our divorce. I
called 911 and stayed inside of the daycare
until the cops came into the building with my
keys in hand. I asked them where my husband

47

was and they explained that he saw them and tried to leave in my car, but they had blocked off the exits. Since I was calling from a daycare, they didn't know if he was going to harm anyone in there. I thanked them and had to rush to the courthouse before I was late getting my divorce. When I got there and talked to my lawyer, I had wanted full custody of our son, but she said it was too late to ask the judge for that. I had it in my paperwork, though, that if I felt my husband would harm our son, he didn't have to go with him, so we left everything as is. Within an hour, I had my divorce, but I didn't feel free. After six years of being with him, I was now single again, but

I didn't know what to do. Yes, I had been apart from him for six months, but I still loved him. I would still see him for sex. He was a good man, I just hated when he would get drunk or high and want to argue over nothing. School, work, and my boys kept me busy, but I still needed – or wanted – companionship. That year was hard. There were two deaths within two months of each other in my ex-husband's family and I was hurt because I loved his family as much as I loved my own. After the second death, I again had to deal with abuse from him. He came over and he had been doing drugs, was drunk, and wanted sex. I didn't. Drunk sex is not

always good sex to me. Even crying didn't
stop him from wanting it, so I did what I
could. Next, I knew, I was throwing up from
crying while trying to perform oral sex on
him. Then I was told to clean it up. The next
day, he came over again, and I don't know
what was up, but he was in a horrible mood.
We started down the street, but my car
messed up and he thought I did something on
purpose. We had to backtrack to the
apartment and I told the boys to go to their
room. I was not sure what was about to
happen, but it wasn't good. He was scaring
me, so I joined the boys in their room and
started trying to push everything I could up

against the door. I was trying to think of what
to do as I was trying to protect us. I had left
the phone in the other room, so I couldn't call
anyone. I decided to just jump out the
window and go get help. He would never
harm the boys, so they would be okay in the
room, but out of all nights, there was no car
to jump down onto, and we lived three floors
up. My next thought was to take off the
window screen to tap on my neighbor's
window, but I guess my ex-husband heard me
doing something and he came to the door and
tried to get in. The boys start crying. We all
were trying to keep him out of the room by
pushing against the dresser I had in front of

the door, but he was stronger than us and
made his way in. Next, I knew, he was tossing
stuff at me and I kept asking him to just leave.
The boys ran out of the room and I started
praying out loud and asking him to stop. I
guess someone must have heard my cry. The
buzzer at the gate was ringing, and he stopped
to go and see who it was before the boys did.
I stayed in the room, praying and crying until
a cop came walking in and asked if I was okay.
I explained what had just taken place while
my ex-husband was saying he didn't know
why I was in there harming myself. The
officers saw the look on my face when he said
that and decided to arrest him for abuse. I was

given a subpoena to appear in court the next

day. It turned out there were about four of us

there for domestic violence, and some people

came to talk to us before we all went into the

courtroom. I was called last to come up, but

sitting there listening to the other ladies, it was

like each was telling my story. We all had been

through the same thing. The judge asked me

why he did what he did, and I said, "You

know, that's a good question. He's sitting over

there. Can we ask him?" Our abusers weren't

allowed to talk, just listen to what they had

done to each of us. When I was in school, I

had to write a paper, and I chose domestic

violence. Some of what I read was true. It said

if you survive your abuser, the system would abuse you next. I had a doctor's appointment around the same time as I was to be in court. I went to the courthouse first, but they were running late, so I went to my doctor's appointment. I'd scheduled it to get an opinion on the blood clot in my arm. My ex-husband had thrown the car seat, and I had blocked it. Since I had a watch on, the blood had nowhere to flow, and the blow caused it to clot up. The doctor cautioned he was going to have to cut it out if it didn't start healing and going away. It looked like it was, though, so he left it in there. Back at the courthouse, they said I was in contempt of court, which merited jail time. I lost my mind. I started

running off at the mouth before the judge

could say they were going to waive that time,

but I needed to come to my next hearing. I

was so relieved. I had work, school, and two

kids to worry about. Jail time was nowhere to

be in there.

February 11, 2000

A new beginning was about to start. My boys and I moved into a new place and I was so excited. I didn't care that all we had there the first night was the TV, VCR, and some sleeping bags. We played camping. Everything else was moved in the next day. I purposely moved further away from my ex-husband, thinking he wouldn't walk that far. Well, I thought wrong. One day, the boys were over at my mom's house since I had gone out clubbing the night before. I guess since I didn't answer my phone around 3 AM, I ended up hearing a knock on my door around 6 or 7 AM. I'm like, "Who could be at my door this early?" Of course, it was my ex-husband. I asked what he was doing there and how did he get there. He had walked all the way to my place from across town. Well, I made that the day I got my backbone straight again. I was going to speak my mind, and if something happened, it happened. At least it wasn't going to happen while my kids were there to witness it. I was allowed to say what I had to say, and then I took him home to his mom's house, just to get him away from my place. I was so proud of myself that day.

April 25, 2001

Internet dating. When you're shy and trying to move on in life, you try almost anything to avoid having to talk to someone face to face right off. I had missed out on a lot of things being shy in my high school and college days. I was too shy to tell a guy I liked him or

wanted to get to know him. I would hope he
would notice me and start talking to me first.
Well, with online dating, you can say hi and
move on to the next profile. If they speak
back, cool. If not, no biggie, move on to the
next. Maybe they'll say hi back. What counted
for me was here you get to know men and try
to meet up later. My downfall on this, though,
is most of the men online aren't in your city
or even your state. Also, you have to be
careful about meeting men online because
they might not always be telling the truth
about themselves or their past. When I felt
comfortable, I would meet a man out
somewhere. I started noticing, though, I was

falling for some kinda fast. I guess you can do that when you've been hurt and treated so badly. Someone saying nice things about you would make you believe almost anything they say. I found myself after a while going from one site to another site to another. I found some great men and some not so great. That didn't matter; I was hooked on these sites. After being on for about two years, I decided to fly and meet someone. I had been chatting with him for a few months and had already met someone from his state before, so I talked to that friend, and since he worked at the airport, I went ahead and made the arrangements to fly and meet the guy. I got my sister to keep my boys while I flew down

to Atlanta, Georgia for a weekend. When I

got there, I contacted my friend since he was

working that night. I told him I was going to

stay right where I was until he could see the

man I was there to meet, that way someone in

Atlanta would know who I was with. I had

already given this guy's info to my sister and

my best friend at the time. Well, let's just say

when I got to where the guy was, he was a

little bigger than his picture showed him to

be. I also found out the next morning that not

only had I been chatting with him, but I had

also been chatting with his best friend. You

see, there were some things that his best

friend and I talked about that sparked my

interest that he and I didn't share. So, I was

bold enough to say I needed to meet his best

friend since we had more in common. Well,

he made sure that his best friend and I would

not be meeting that weekend. So needless to

say, that was not a great weekend for me in

Atlanta. I ended up having to stay an extra

night in town because there was snow in

Kansas City, Missouri preventing me from

flying home. When my friend from the airport

got off of work, he met up with me at the

hotel that the airline had put me up in and

showed me the town. It made me want to see

more since I got the quick look of the town

and since it was dark out, I really couldn't see much of the city like I wanted to. I flew home the next morning and never contacted the misleading man again, but I did make plans to go back to Atlanta later that year. My boys and I went down over Thanksgiving weekend and had a nice time. From there, it became a hope of mine to one day move to Atlanta. A few years later, I decided to trust someone else and go for a visit to New York, New York. We used to talk so long on the phone; one night I think it was five hours. He called me after I had left a club and next I knew the sun was coming up. I'm like, oh boy, I'm going to be so tired. I knew my boys would be

getting up soon and would want something to
eat. I was glad that by now the boys were
older and could do a lot on their own, so if I
needed to take a nap, I could do so without
having to wonder what they were doing. By
the next year, we made the plans, and off to
New York I went for Valentine's Day
weekend. It was a very nice trip with lots of
site seeing. He gave me a gift and I was all
smiles. I'm not really sure what happened
after that trip, though. We remained friends
but just didn't talk as much. One year, I fell
for someone from Mississippi, but this time
instead of me going to see him, I allowed him
to come and see me. It was a very nice visit.

He met my boys, my best friend who went with me to get him from the airport, and eventually he met my mom. She wanted me to meet her at the mall, and since we were out eating, I didn't have time to go and drop him off at my place. We went out to the lake and took some pictures. That wasn't something I had done with anyone else, so I was feeling some type of way by the time he had to leave. The weekend was so nice, I wasn't ready for it to be over. Something happened after that trip, and we didn't talk much. Still, it was at a moment in my life where I was in the process of planning to move out of the state of Kansas. If something could have happened with us, I would have moved to Mississippi. If

not, then I would move on to Atlanta. So, I

ended up in Atlanta.

March 1, 2003

This was the day God brought me someone

that would become a safe haven in my life.

She and her boyfriend were putting on a male

revue and I was posting stuff on a page I

made on a site called Black Planet. I called her

up and asked if it was okay to post their show

on my page to try and get the word out to

others that might not know about the show from them just passing out flyers. She agreed, and we ended up talking for like an hour or so, even though we both were at work. It turned out she was a cousin of my ex-husband's, which made her a cousin to my second son. We decided to meet up and talked some more. She ended up asking me to help with the show – which ended up being only the second male revue I had ever been to. I got to meet one of the dancers I had been chatting with on a dating site. He was as cool in person as he was online, and a very good dancer. I was invited to hang with her and some of her friends for another show in another city. Even though I was a little shy to be around people I didn't know, I went and had a good time. From there, I helped them with other shows and I would visit her any time I was in town since she didn't live in Topeka. She had become my best friend. She had given me a makeover and I was so grateful for her and her boyfriend for the show they held for me on my 35th birthday. They took my two dancers and a few friends and added 10 dancers and many other guests. It was so great, and it was the first time I didn't have to really plan my own birthday party. Eventually, she ended up moving to Topeka, and I was so happy I could see her more often. Outside of helping with parties, I would help her with her and her sister's hair salon and boutique. This after working at the middle school and checking on my boys every day. It was a good way for me to relieve my stress. This friend showed me things that ladies do together. I hadn't gone shopping with others, or gotten my nails done, and she gave me my first pair of open-toed shoes. She also introduced me to weaves and wigs when my hair was coming out a lot. I had made a doctor's appointment to have my situation checked out, but until then, she had to convince me on the wigs. At first, I was against them since all I knew about them was that people wore them on TV. I was afraid it might fly off in the wind. So, my friend helped me pick out a wig, and I must have been wearing it good, because the receptionist didn't realize I had one on. I had to take it off for the doctor to look at my scalp and he wanted to run some tests to see why the patch of hair was gone and not really growing back. The results were that I didn't have cancer, but Scarred Alopecia. This meant I would be losing most, if not all, of my hair. He gave me some cortisone shots in my head. Can we say OUCH??!! He numbed the area with ice and then gave me little shots in my scalp where the hair was gone to see if it would grow back.

75

It was either the ten little shots or one big one, so I made my decision. Well, some time went by and that didn't work. I didn't want to keep getting the shots in my head, so I just decided to deal with the fact that one day I wouldn't have my own hair. I knew I could just keep wearing the wigs and my friend could keep giving me braids and weaves until I didn't have enough hair to get them anymore. Her motto was, "If I can grab it, I can braid it." Our friendship felt more like a sisterhood than friends. I love her so much for showing me what it was like to have a female friend.

April 24, 2007

I was prepared, but not ready for this day. My Dad was called home to preach for the Lord. You see, I got a call on Valentine's Day about him not doing well, I prayed that God would let Dad stick around until my spring break from work. Then my boys and I could drive down and see him. God heard my prayer. During our spring break, we drove down to

Mississippi and spent time with Dad and the family, and did some sightseeing when he wasn't up for visitors. We had a good time the last night in town, but it was also a time that I dreaded. When I was about to leave, Dad grabbed my hand, and even though he didn't say anything aloud, he said plenty in that touch. It was just weird to hear him so quiet. When you have a preacher for a dad, he has plenty to say. During that last visit, he didn't say much at all. Dad had Alzheimer's, and it was getting close to the end. We went back home, and a month later, around three something in the morning, I got a call that he had passed away. Since Dad was a preacher for a long time, it took a moment for his

funeral to be arranged, giving me time to

prepare for my trip back to Mississippi to say

my goodbyes. The funeral was huge, and a

little over four hours long. I got to meet a lot

of family, and it was the first time all of my

living siblings and I were together since we

met. Our brother Terry was the only one

missing, but he had passed away six years

prior. I wrote a tribute to my dad about how I

felt about him. Since I didn't get to see him as

much as everyone else, I saw him as the long-

distance phone call and so I wrote him a letter

about it.

"The Long-Distance Call"

As I was growing up, all I really knew was

to just call you when I needed to talk.

When I wanted something, I was told to

just call. When I was ready to meet the

siblings that I didn't know, all I had to do

was call. When we talked, we exchanged

80

our hurts and pains, but it wasn't to complain. It was our way of communicating that we understood what the other was going through. Even though I didn't grow up in your house, when I would visit, I was not treated like an outsider. I was accepted like I fit right in there. I felt like I grew up with the rest. I thank you dad and Willa Mae for welcoming me every time I wanted to come and stay. My last visit I will remember most, because of the touch of your hand. you held on as if you didn't want to let go. We didn't say much, but through that touch, we said a lot. So, dad, to me you will always be that long-

distance call. even though you are not

here in the present, all I have to do is call

your name and you will still be that long-

distance call away. I love you, dad, then,

now, and forever."

Your Daughter,

Pamela Harmon-Porter

May 19, 2007

I prayed for this day ever since my firstborn

entered the school system. With him having

ADHD, it was a stressful task to get him to

focus. I had to go to the school extra to get

on him about getting stuff done. He would

complain about teachers in his high school

days to where I actually sat in all of his classes

just like I was a student. Classes during those days were split, so it took me two days to go to all of them. I found out it wasn't the teachers, it actually was him not paying attention in class. He would space out if the subject was boring to him. His graduation day was a glorious day to see. I wanted to be up there on that stage with him since it took me all these years to keep him on task. My mom's companion had bought him his suit for graduation since that's something he said he would do for him if he graduated. Afterward, we had a nice dinner for him at my mom's house.

September 6, 2008

I stepped out in faith and moved from Topeka, Kansas to Decatur, Georgia. I had never lived anywhere else but Kansas, and this was a very scary decision, but I knew God had me. The complex didn't have my apartment ready when I got there and the friend that helped me come down put me up in a hotel for a couple days. After that, I stayed with him and his family in an extended stay hotel.

After a week, my apartment was "ready." I

don't know how they could claim this,

because when I got in there, I found at least

12 things wrong. Luckily, I hadn't moved my

things down yet. Within three days of being in

my apartment, I was ready to move.

Compared to where I had been living in

Topeka for the past eight plus years, that

place was straight ghetto. The kids were rude

and so very disrespectful. Since we don't have

trains in Kansas, it took me close to a month

to get on the Marta train. There was a football

game with black bands playing and I wanted

to go, so to the train I went. Luckily, so did

thousands of others, so it was easy to figure

out that day. I'm glad I did because the game

and bands were great and I had to start getting

on the train more as I needed to find a job. I

didn't find one until about three months later,

and it was good I did because I was running

out of money. I had now moved my youngest

son down and he had to get the school

supplies he needed, so my savings went kinda

fast. The job was pretty easy. I just didn't like

the long commute via train to get there. It

took me like an hour and a half to get to

work, when if I had still had my car, it would

have taken me 30 minutes. Unfortunately, my

car broke down right before I was to move to

Georgia. After my son had been there for about two months, he was not liking it and had threatened to run away. I was scared to go to work, thinking when I came home he might not be there. With the way my hours were set up, we left around the same time and got home around the same time also. Eventually, I had to call my mom and ask her if my son could live with her until I got things better in Georgia. She said yes, and back to Kansas he went. I had never lived without my kids since they were born, and now I was all alone for the first time in my life. I had lived with my mom, my oldest son, my ex-husband, or both my sons. Never had I lived alone. It was a little scary at first, but after a while, I got used to it. I feel that it helped me really grow up.

June 10, 2009

On this day, I ran into a man that I'd been

getting to know a little at a time. We had run

into each other at Five Points Station a few

times prior to this. I guess he had been

noticing me, but I hadn't noticed him until he

asked me how many books I read a week.

Since my commute to work was so long, I

would read books to pass the time away. I

told him, depending on the book, I could read one and start another one within the same week. Since he usually got off the train after two stops, our talks were short. One day, I was waiting on a train at Georgia State Station and he showed up there (he was headed to the store, he said), but this time he had to do a doubletake because I was not in my usual work clothes that he was used to seeing me in. That day I had on a nice sundress. We chatted for a little bit until he got off the train a couple stops before me. So now, there I was, going to the library, and guess who I saw at a table. Since there would be a little bit of a wait for a computer, I signed in and went back to

the table to talk to him for a moment until his
number came up to go use a computer. That
day, he gave me his name, number, and email
address. So, in return, I did the same. The
funny thing was, I was checking my emails
when I got on the computer and there was
one from him while we were in the library
still. From that day forward, a friendship
began. We would talk and text via phone and
he would email me sometimes also. He
seemed to be a very nice man. One day, he
had gotten tickets to see the Atlanta Dreams
play basketball. Of course, not really being
from Atlanta, I didn't know who they were, so
he told me it was Atlanta's WNBA team.

Since the game was at 7 PM and during those days I got off work at 2:30 PM, I said sure I would love to go. So, after work, I rushed home to clean up and change. I told him I would just meet him at the venue since we still didn't know where each other lived. Later I found out we lived only three train stops away from each other. He waited for me outside the Phillips Arena. We had some pretty nice seats since his friend's daughter played basketball and her team was given tickets to go to the game. I got to meet some of his friends, who were from his high school and college days. They all were pretty nice to me. It was a good outing with good company.

After about a month of getting to know each other, he gave me his address and asked me to meet him at his place. It turned out we lived only three train stops away from each other. He got off a little later than me, so I went home to change and took the train to his place. He had left me the key to get in, and I was like, Hmmm, seems pretty trusting to let someone he's still getting to know in his place like it's not possible to have a woman rob him. That night, we chatted while he made dinner for us and we watched TV. He was a pretty good cook and tried to always cook healthy meals. That was different for me since I cooked more southern meals. We got to

95

know each other more during the dinner since it was just us in a more relaxing place. When it got late, he walked me back to the train station where we said our goodnights. I informed him when I made it home safe, and went to bed. My kids came down to visit in July, and since he and I weren't a couple, I didn't invite him over to meet them. Every day after work, I tried to do something with them around town. Well, on that Saturday, we were at a mall. Since it was the boys' last night in town and he was in the area, I asked him to just come meet up with us for dinner. It was a little awkward when it was time to go, though. My kids had never really seen me with anyone since my divorce. When we were saying bye at the train station, we had to go two different directions, so we gave each other a quick hug and parted ways. He was a very nice man, and since I was still new to town, he would take me places and we would do things, hang out with his friends, and go to games together. We started hanging out at each other's place to a point where I ended up asking him were we a couple, and he said yes. You see, I was used to the man asking you to be his lady. These were the days where if you're hanging out a lot, that just makes you a couple and although I knew that, I still needed my question answered. It had been 12 years since

I had a boyfriend, but it was nice to have someone again. Our age difference didn't bother me much, but there were other times when it did bother me. It reminded me of my parents, and my mom's age difference with her companion. My guy was a little younger than my mom, but since he could keep up with me, I let it go and saw him for him. I loved that he loved to go dancing and just hang out. One other thing I noticed was I was a giver of things and he wasn't. That didn't bother me as much until Christmas. I had to work that day and so I spent the night at his place so we could at least spend Christmas morning together. I brought over my gifts for him and I didn't look to see if he had gifts for me. The morning came and I was excited like a little kid, but then sadness took over just as fast. He had no gifts for me, none and it hurt when people who knew I had a man asked, "So what did you get?" and I had to say, "Nothing." Then they said, "NOTHING?" I got breakfast, I guess you can say, but oh well. His birthday was in a couple months, and I had arranged for us to attend the 70s Soul Jam concert a few weeks after it. The day of his birthday, I took him to dinner and a movie. For some reason, Christmas kept getting to me and I started thinking this wasn't going to work. There were some other issues, but I

99

didn't really want to go into that. We had a

good time at the concert and the next month I

had the tell him about how I felt about

everything. When he told me he loved me, I

didn't know if he was just saying that because

I was breaking up with him or he really meant

it because he had never said those words to

me before. I told him I really didn't want to

lose him as a friend, so friends we were. We

actually were pretty good as friends. He even

opened up more to me after that. Then

something happened, someone came back

into his life and it took him a couple of

months to tell me about it. He had a few baby

mamas. Even though all his kids but one was

grown, he didn't really see them, just the second son and his last son. Well, the first baby mama came back into his life because their grown son was now sick and he wasn't expecting to live past a year. I was all for him to get to know this son and spend as much time with him as possible. It wasn't like we were a couple, we were just friends, but for some reason, he started confiding in me less. The day that he asked me to ride down with him to see his son in the hospital was the day I discovered I fell in love with him. I didn't realize it until I felt something was going on between him and his first baby mama. You see, us Cancers have this sixth sense about some things, and there was something going on in that hospital that didn't include me. I found myself alone a lot with their son in his hospital room while they were who knows where. I know it was an upsetting time, but why not tell me what's up? On the way back home, I decided to ask him. He claimed there was nothing going on, but did say others had asked that also. I let it go until I kept getting this feeling I was about to lose him and I didn't like it. If only I would have accepted that I was in love with him and realized that the fact that he wasn't a giver wasn't as important as everything else we had going on, she wouldn't have been a threat to me losing my friend. I chose to write my feelings down and give them to him, but by then, I had been chatting with their son via Facebook and he told me things I didn't want to hear. I had to face the reality that he had moved on but for some reason wasn't able to tell me this to my face no matter how many times I asked him. It was hard to get past this, but I did. I was like, "As long as we can still be friends we're good," and he said, "We will never give up our friendship."

April 27, 2010

This was a very hard day for me at work. I found out my friend of nine years had passed away. We talked all the time, day or night, and I had just told him about my aunt passing in Mississippi the week before. He had said that he hurt himself at work and was home resting. Well, all of a sudden, he wasn't responding to my calls or text messages, and he wasn't on Facebook like he used to be. I was getting very worried. I even made a joke in one text, asking if I should be looking for him in the obituaries, not knowing I was right on the money with that statement. You see, this night I was at work, and a guy was walking around asking people did they know this person he had on his phone. So, I decided to be nosey and look at the picture he was showing. I asked why he was asking people if they know him and he said because my friend just passed away. My heart just dropped. I tried to keep it together since I still had a few hours to work, but I was close to losing it. I went upstairs for some privacy as I started crying. He was only 44 years old. It turned out he had a stroke or heart attack while at work and didn't tell me how serious it was. Next, I got another blow to find out the lady I thought was his live-in ex-girlfriend was actually his wife. I knew everything about him but the fact that he had married this lady. I had so many questions, but I guess those questions will never be answered now. I wanted to attend his wake, but since I didn't want to go alone, I just went to his funeral with another friend that used to work with him. It turned out there were a lot of females that didn't know he had a wife. Regardless, I will always have a place in my heart for him. He helped me in more ways than he'll ever know.

December 5, 2010

Well, by now, my ex chose to be with his first

baby mama, and even though she wanted him

to cut ties with me, we decided against that.

He told her she couldn't pick his friends, but I

guess she thought since he wouldn't let our

friendship go, she'd take matters into her own

hands. I had just gotten back from visiting a

friend in Baltimore, Maryland, and decided to

go watch a football game with him on my way home. We were having a laughing good time when I got an alert on my phone that I had a Facebook message. Guess who it was from. I read it and said, "Wow, your lady just inboxed me," and right after I read him what it said, she just happened to call him. Now, I'm thinking this would be a good time for him to question her about it, but he chose not. I, of course, questioned him about it when he got off of the phone. He claimed he didn't want to start an argument, which meant they must have been arguing over me and him not letting our friendship go. You see, she was at his place one day while he was at work, and unlike me, she decided to roam his place looking for evidence. I guess she was looking for evidence that we were more than just friends since we used to go together. So, during her search, she found the letters I wrote him and some other stuff that he kept that I had given him like some CDs I made for him while we were a couple. In her message, she tried to be nice in addressing a few issues concerning me and him, which mind you, me and him have none. It was the two of them who had the issues. Anyway, she claimed they had been together for eight months and my confession of love for him was a form of disrespect. Hmm. Well, at the time, they were not an item, and eight months prior would have been around the time I had just broken up with him and she came back into his life. Was she trying to say just because they met up, he became hers? But instead of me replying to her, I was going to let him take care of it. Well, I guess since we didn't end our friendship still, she decided two weeks later to contact me again. I again chose to ignore her and let him talk to her. Well, that must not have worked because while I was feeling down on Christmas day, here comes another message from her. I had had enough of being silent, so I let her have it. If you have trust in your relationship, there is no need to snoop in your partner's phone, email, inbox,

mailbox, or anything else, but she was in all of

his stuff and only saw what she wanted to see.

She didn't care that I was replying to what he

was saying or asking me. She only cared about

what I would say to him. I got to a point to

where I felt if he didn't care about his

relationship, why should I? I told him to be

honest with that lady and me, but from what I

saw, he couldn't even be honest with himself.

I kept telling them both I didn't want him

back, I just wanted our friendship because

that was what we had before we even became

a couple. We were good friends and were

going to continue to be good friends. We

never argued, we talked like the grown adults we were. She, on the other hand, was a feisty old lady. She was 55 years old and always trying to fight a 41-year old. All I could see was that she was a control freak and mad because her man was not doing as she demanded. She stole a CD I gave him, took a Christmas card out of his mailbox that I sent him, stole my phone number out of his phone, and since I blocked them both from my Facebook, she started trying to email me through his email address. She wrote me a few letters, broke up the CD she stole, tore up the card, and mailed it all to me. Then she was dumb enough to call and leave a voicemail

saying she did it.

Smile Through It All

July 13, 2012

This was my first full day in Miami, Florida with a group of people going down for some fun. I had decided to be adventurous and go with. They went every year, and since it was my birthday weekend, I decided to save up my money and go with them. We left Atlanta the night of July 11th and arrived in Miami on my

birthday afternoon, aka July 12th. I got to

finally meet a man I had known for 10 years.

He was the one who told me about these

people that traveled to Miami every year. It

was so nice to finally see him and hang out for

my birthday. When I went back to our hotel, I

started chatting with one of my roommates

for the trip. No one knew I was bald yet since

I'd worn a wig thus far, but I knew we would

be getting in the pool eventually and I

couldn't wear it then. I can't control how

people act, but I can control when they find

out. I asked my roommate, "How do I look?"

and took off the wig. I was a little scared at

118

first of what she might say, but she said I

looked good. So I smiled, thanked her, and

the next morning, I gave myself a fresh shave

and we went to have breakfast with the rest of

the group. A lot of them were shocked that I

was bald and asked what happened. I said I

just took the wig off and that I had actually

been bald for years. I was feeling confident

that weekend, I guess, so after breakfast, I

asked a friend to take a picture of me. I

posted it on my Facebook page and we went

about our day. We went to the beach,

shopping, and I just tried to not wonder if

anyone was looking at my head. When we got

back to the hotel room that night, I looked at

my Facebook page and I just started crying from all of the positive comments. Some were concerned, and it took me a minute to understand why. They thought I had cancer and I had to explain that I actually had alopecia. When we came back to Atlanta, my son and I went out to eat to celebrate my birthday. When we were about to leave, he said, "Mom, you're forgetting something." I asked him what it was and he said, "Your wig." See, before, I wouldn't even answer my door without grabbing a wig first. I wouldn't walk to check the mailbox without a wig on. I was truly afraid to show that I had no hair, but I had seen a lot of bald women around town. I thought, if they can do it, so can I. So I told him, "Mama has to get used to leaving home without the wigs." Going to work for the first time was a test. I got asked as soon as I walked in, what did I do? Why did I cut my hair? Then some said it looked good. My male best friend had shown me how to completely shave my head, and now I had to do it more often if I was going to be leaving the apartment without my wigs. Some bald men even asked me for shaving tips after a while, which makes me laugh. Walking around bald has its ups and downs. Some women are like how I was, afraid to reveal their heads, and some give great compliments on how nice I look bald. Some say, "Everyone can't pull off that look, but it's sexy on you." I never knew how many men are attracted to bald women until I took off the wigs. I've been called a stud, sir, young man, bro since coming out of the wigs. I try to wear hoop earrings more often now, but at work, I can't wear them, so I try to wear lipstick a lot. I don't wear makeup really, so my simple look is what you get. It took some time to get used to the stares and the assumptions, but I can now joke about my baldness and I think it's so freeing and sexy. I dress up every chance I get and I take the stares with confidence now.

November 21, 2012

This is a day I had been waiting on for six months. I met face to face with who I thought was my future husband. We had known each other for eight years via the internet and we used to talk a lot online and on the phone. We never really thought about getting together to become a couple, though, until earlier that year. He used to post comments on my pictures on Facebook, and one of my sisters had said we would make a great couple. We thought about it for a moment and started talking more. That year I had done a lot, traveled a lot, and stepped outside of the box a lot. I was trying to deal with my youngest being back in Georgia and going to school. Then a friend came down with his son and we tried to see where that would go, but with dealing with a teen, a 23-year-old, a job that I didn't like working nights at, and now a friend and his autistic son was too much for me. I was not used to being around a child with Autism. I didn't know how to handle him. Plus, I was the only female in the house. So

needless to say, my stress level was very high.
I had to sadly tell my friend he had to find
somewhere else to go, not knowing he would
decide to go back to Virginia. I drove back
there with him and his son. It was a nice little
trip in which I met his family and decided to
go back for a visit a month or so later. I just
wished he had stayed in Georgia so we could
have seen if things could work out. I really
liked him and wanted to try a relationship
with him, but I needed a little time to figure
stuff out. That year, for my birthday, I also
went to Miami for the first time on a party
bus with some people I knew. I got to finally
meet a friend I'd been chatting with for 10

years. While I was in Miami, I also had to learn that my friend from Virginia had decided to get back with his ex. That hit me hard, but I had started talking to my friend in California more and saw that we had a lot more in common than we had given notice to. So, we made plans to meet face to face finally. I was falling for him the more we talked and I couldn't wait to get to California. The trip was very nice, and we decided to become a couple while I was there. I also met his mom and best friend. Plus, I got to spend some time with one of my cousins that lived out there who I hadn't seen since my aunt's funeral two years prior. After a week, I went back home

and was sad to leave him, but we made plans
for me to come back for a visit that next
February for 2 weeks. It was nice to spend
time in California. I loved the beaches, going
to San Francisco, and taking a lot of pictures.
There was something wrong with my
relationship, though. We kept arguing over
little stuff. I had to decide whether to
continue with this relationship or let it go.
Long-distance was hard, but I chose to stay in
the relationship to try and make it work. We
made more plans. This time, he was to come
and see me in Atlanta, but that got changed to
him meeting up with me in Kansas for his
birthday and my youngest son's graduation

since it was the same weekend. Well, that

meet up didn't happen either, but I was to go

to California again to try out living there.

May 18, 2013

This is a day I dreamed of happening that almost didn't; my youngest son's graduation day. He had dropped out for a little bit, but with prayer and lot of talks, we got him to go back. There were some other things that almost stopped this day, but again, prayer works. He still had to attend summer school to get his diploma, but he got to walk with his class and finish high school on time. I'm so proud of him. I don't talk to his dad any more since he's gotten re-married, and since our son doesn't wish to see him, we didn't invite him to celebrate this milestone with us. My older son and I also ran into his dad at two of his daughters' graduations a few hours before my son's graduation and we almost didn't talk to him. Neither one of my kids grew to like their fathers, but it's their fathers' fault since they didn't try to be more of a dad to either one of them. I guess other things were more important, but I never talked bad about their dads to them and I let them chose their own

path when it came to their dads or life
choices. I was in town for a month, so my son
and I got to spend some time together before
I went on to California to try to see if I would
be moving there with my boyfriend. Well,
after three weeks, I had to make the hard
decision to go back home to Georgia. I just
couldn't make this relationship work no
matter how much I wanted it to. There was
still a lot of arguing and disagreements and I
was just feeling like I was being controlled.
After being in an abusive marriage, I couldn't
think of being in a relationship where I felt
like I had no say. It was like everything I did
was not right or good enough. It all had to be

his decision or his way. Leaving him was one of the hardest things I had to do. I felt we were right for each other, but maybe not. I am very happy we worked things out to remain friends though.

September 23, 2015

My ex-boyfriend from California finally came to see me in Atlanta. It had been about 30 years since he had been there, but out of all the times he told me he was coming, he finally made it, and then I was reminded why we weren't a couple. That control was back, the arguing was back. I don't know why he felt that nothing would go right if someone else suggested something to do or another way of doing things. He wasn't feeling too good during this trip, so we made the best of it. We went sightseeing and out to eat a couple times. We had some good talks before he had to leave town. Part of me really wanted to get back with him if things would have gone better, but I think we're just meant to stay good friends. To this day, he really cares about and loves me, as I do him, and that means a lot to me.

April 13, 2016

I decided to get into another long-distance relationship with a nice-looking man from Chicago, Illinois. He had sent me a message on Facebook on August 22, 2015, and we talked for eight months before we decided to meet in person. We learned we had a lot in common and wanted a lot of the same things for our future. I had needed a break from Georgia, so I told him I would go to Chicago instead of having him come to Georgia for our first meeting. I hadn't been to Chicago since I was 12 when I went there for a family reunion. We talked about everything that was going on in our lives; exes, kids, family, and how we wanted better in our lives. I really fell for him before we met, but I kept my feelings cool until we spent those first few days together. We went sightseeing and just spent time together until it was time for me to go back home. Before I left, he asked me to be his lady, and I said yes. Later, I got hit up on my Facebook messenger from a few women that knew him. I had commented on his

Memorial Day post, and my profile picture

was of us on the day I left Chicago. One of

the women claimed she was also his woman

and asked if I was his woman or his cousin,

which he had told them I was. I questioned

him on why four different women asked me if

I was his cousin. He claimed they were trying

to be messy, and it took some convincing, but

I let it go. He traveled to Georgia in July for

my birthday. Then I went back to Chicago in

September. In December, he came back to

visit me again. I thought we would have

gotten to spend more time together, but he

said he had to go see his brother in Dallas.

Somehow, he ended up at some lady's house that he had claimed was his cousin. This got me to thinking about the women that thought I was his cousin. Plus, he was supposed to go back to Chicago to spend Christmas with his daughter, but I came to find out he was still in Dallas. Hmm. Well, after a lot of thinking, I chose to go to Chicago one last time for Valentine's Day. It was like he was trying to get me to not come because he didn't have a lot of money to do much, but I'm a romantic and wanted to be with my man on that day. When I got there, it felt like we weren't a couple anymore. I spent most of my time in his room watching TV, and he spent his time in the living room watching TV. I kept asking were we going to get out and do something, and he claimed we were. Then he would wait so late he would end up saying that we might not be able to make it back to the house because we had to take public transportation. Thinking about how late he'd be out when I wasn't in town or he would have someone's car, this wasn't adding up to me. Just like he would be around friends when I wasn't in town, but when I was in town, they were nowhere to be found. So, with these comparisons, I had plenty to think about and I told him if he really wanted this relationship to work, he would do better to try and keep it.

I left town February 18, 2017, and haven't been back to Chicago since. I broke it off a month later. We're still friends, but I don't think I will ever trust him again. I was really hurt after this because I really thought he was different. I told him how other men had done me and he turned around and did the same. I truly believe he had a relationship with me in Atlanta while having one with another woman in Chicago. I don't think I want another long-distance relationship after this. This last relationship really has me thinking, what am I doing wrong? Or is it the men I choose?

July 01, 2020

I find myself in deep thought about my past; a past that I am no longer bound by. A past that I have ultimately been freed from and I reflect on what it has been just to let everyone know that they are not alone. I have suffered through everything from the vows being broken, to depression, to suicidal thoughts, to experiences with substance abusers and abusers in general, to scandals, to the discovery of

141

alopecia, to the fear of Alzheimer, to the battles with self-love and self-confidence, to issues with loneliness, to self-sabotage, to the lack of support and reciprocation, to divorce, to bad decision making, to financial issues, to constant relocation, to the transitioning of dear loved ones, to raising a child who has ADHD, to the challenges with online dating, and ultimately to the ups and downs; peaks and valleys of this journey. However, despite all of that I can still smile. I have to say that prayer truly works and you too can be freed from the things that hold you back from being your best self. As I continue to walk through this journey called life, pursue purpose, love myself, accomplish goals, and wait for true love, I will continue to be thankful that I have been and am able to "SMILE THROUGH IT ALL."

Family & Friends

Dance Pam Dance,

Have you ever seen Pam dance or listen to her share a conversation about her past relationship or about alopecia?
Her dancing and conversation will remind you of a beautiful flower, like a Lily. Who sways with the gentlest breeze and knows how
to stand planted in the storms of life's journeys. She always looks you in your eyes when you are talking with her and lets you know what you are convening is important no matter how silly or stressful one sound.

When we first met she glided across the floor reporting for work. Having a conversation or hellos for everyone and if she had an issue with you it wasn't long before you knew it and the issue(s) was resolved. My first thoughts before our greeting "why did she shave her hair off, it going to be soon cold or is she going thru that awful chemo?

Her head neatly shaped and glowing, her face very pretty and that Smile said I'm okay or you? I couldn't ask for a better colleague. Pam is very Dependable and always learning, whether it's about people, the next production, things in life, or economic situation. Pam is a conversationalist. I often pictured her as the little girl who always had conversations in class

143

especially when it was a quiet time. I wouldn't be able to live with issues she has encountered.

They say Joy comes in the morning however Pam has Joy with her 24/7. Pam doesn't let alopecia (during one of the talks she told me about alopecia) to define her or keep her in bondage. She displays Rest when she talks about the harsh times or harsh people and this lets me know she trusts in GOD.
and if you are familiar with Dr. Martin Luther King quote, *" I have decided to stick with LOVE. Hate is too great a burden to bear".* *then you will love Pam, what's not to love about her, alopecia doesn't have her.*

I.H.S. I am Free
  de'Lores

Kelli Cay (Childhood friend): You have always been amazing to me even as a kid, you didn't judge, you were caring, and mannn you had an infectious laugh, lol..but mostly you were kind even then.

Corebin Porter (Son): You are caring and kind, a great mother, supportive, sweet, always straight forward, and a good person.

Fred Walton (Friend): You are a good person with a heart of gold. We've been friends for a long time and hanging out with you is always a highlight. You're a person who put time into people and willing to go above and beyond which is a great quality of yours. You re a hard worker. You are resourceful.

144

You have a lot of goals and I hope that you have the opportunity each and every last one them. Keep your head up and your heart open.

Marlon Harmon (Son): I have a lovely mother that is sweet, honest, caring and supportive on things we want to do and become in life and is willing to help us achieve our goals.

Gloria Pledger (Family friend): I met you Pam when I was new to Topeka, KS. You, with your bashful self, your mother, and your sister lived in the other side of the duplex that my mother, father, daughter and I moved into. We all grew to be more than neighbors. We became like family, and then I was the babysitter, as your mother worked the evening shift. Pam, you and your sister would spend your evenings with my family, and kept my daughter La-Toya "Toya" well entertained, until it was homework, and then bedtime. As years came and went, we moved to different addresses, but always had those family ties. Babysitter to hairdresser, and fellow parishioners of the same church, I watched you and your sister grow up and maneuver your ways through life, sometimes the hard way, but not always by your doing. When I look at and think of you, my heart smiles, because I see a well-adjusted, well rounded woman...in spite of the not so good hands that were dealt you at times. Pam, I am so proud to be able to say that I've known you through the years. You are one BRAVE & RESILIENT WOMAN...YES, PHENOMINAL, I would say, because in spite of all of the obstacles that you have faced." YOU HAVE SMILED THROUGH IT ALL" I can't wait to purchase my own copy of "Smile Through It All", and have you personally autograph it for me when you are home again. LIVE LONG AND PROSPER! TO THINE OWN SELF BE TRUE! FLY HIGH GIRL! I LOVE YA PAM!

Annie Harmon (Mother): Pam, I am proud of you. You have come a long way. Keep pushing and put God first. Always love yourself! Be happy! I love you!

Mom!

Lisa Patterson (Cousin): Pam is a very caring, loving, outgoing person who loves her family and friends. Pam is a person that when you meet her she will make you feel special. She will give you her last. When you meet Pam you have met a friend who will stick with you through it all. Love you Pam

Mahalia Watson (Sister): Greetings: I have known author, Pamela Harmon-Porter, most of my life, as she is my sister! The retelling of her hardships has yielded the AMAZING testament of her resilience. When many would have given up, she chose to keep going, which makes me Godly proud and encouraged to keep going--smiling the whole way through.

Charles Yarbrough (Friend): I remember the first day we met in person after meeting online. I admire your openness and digged your laughter. Back then I thought we had forever on our side so we both kinda drug our feet. as time continue to pass and it waits for no one, we continue to grow closer in our

146

friendship. but farther from ever having a Relationship I once thought we would have forever. But life is funny like that. For some reason I always believed we would be together as a couple and that we still had time but yet time continue to pass us by and we even lost touch with each other's for years... when we finally reconnected years later. We we're different still friends but different in our views and directions. I love you and always will because how you captured my eyes and thoughts from the very first time I saw you. With all that said, congratulation on the release of your book, I'm sure everyone that reads it will enjoy it. I'm definitely looking forward to it in my hands. Also, I think that anything is possible because I believe forever lives in us all... hey I may not have gotten the wife I once thought I would have in you ... but I did gain a true friendship between us that will live forever. thank you and again Congratulations.... **C.Y.**

Staceyrene Daniels (Friend): I can't wait to read your book! Ur a sweet, kind, n loving person.

Oceanus Picou (Friend): A very, warm, beautiful, caring, sensual woman who like so many of us just wants to be loved and respected. Pam is the type of woman that most men desire to be with, but often don't do the things to keep her. She has always been a great mother and a good friend. **OS Picou**

Renee Watson (Sister): Hello Pam, I am Renee' Watson, your sister. You are a great single mother who tries every day to make it a better day than before. You have a heart of gold and tries to be there for anyone. Stay encouraged. Love you.

Jamal Williams (Friend): To whom it may concern, my name is Jamal and I have known Pam since about 2003. From the time I have known Pam she has been a great friend and a very caring person. Pam takes all of her friendships seriously

and she is truly loyal and dedicated to each of them. I have known her to mail out cards for birthdays, and she always willing to attend or support a friend's event or business. I witness her display of strength and courage with her move from Kansas to Atlanta barely knowing anyone. I appreciate Pam's friendship and glad I met her.

Jonathan Usher (Friend): Pam, it's been well over 10 years knowing you and I appreciate your friendship and warmth. When others have slighted me, you were there to listen. Even when we disagreed, you were kind and respectful in our disagreement. I appreciate your efforts taken to achieve your longtime goals of writing this book. You adapted to many life challenges and changes, moving from one side of America to another. Maintaining positivity and self-awareness. You are someone whom other's will take from your experience and words; subconsciously encouraging them to do the same to make themselves whole again. You are equal to treatment to everyone, sometimes at fault. For this reason, amongst many, I am always grateful that you call me friend. Take care and stay true to yourself.

Machele Holder (Childhood Friend): To whom it may concern, my name is Machele Logan Holder. I've known Pam since junior high school and reconnected within the last few years in Atlanta. She continues to be a person with integrity, loyalty and compassion. She's an amazing woman, hardworking and incredible friend who has proven she's only a phone call away. After enduring and overcoming all of the challenges throughout her life, she has risen in every sense of the word a true SURVIVOR.

Cece Watson (Baby sister): Pam is a beautiful, and sweet woman who loves to laugh, hang out and have fun. She is a hard worker just like our dad. She has always been a go getter even when life got hard. She never gives up, always keep the faith in God and smile through every challenge and for that, I am beyond elated to call her my big sister. I love you always and forever.

CeCe Watson – Baby Sister

Eric Taylor Sr. (Friend): Pam is an intelligent woman with a beautiful spirit. She is a very loving and kind person. She goes out of her way to make other people feel comfortable and important. I have known Pam for around 10 years and I have never heard her talk down to or about other people. To sum it up Pam is a woman that you would be blessed to have as a friend.

Leon Maben (Friend): Hey Pamela Porter, this is Leon Maben we met about eleven years ago, in the Five Points MARTA Train Station. Congratulations on the writing of your first book. I can't wait to read your book; the title is so intriguing. You were always reading a book on your way to work when I would see you in the train station so writing one is no surprise to me. I believe that's what attracted me to you along with bumping into you all the time in the Decatur Library. Even though there is a big gap between us in age you surprise me with your maturity and conversation. Good luck and I know that & Smile Through It All will do well because you deserve it!!!!

Good Luck, Leon Maben

Archer Casey (Photographer friend): I have
known Pam for over twelve years, she has been a kind thoughtful person, you would never have known the journey she has undergone unless she had chosen to tell you. Strong and determined to not be held hostage by her past she is living testimony of the ability to be free and grow from adversity. A TRUE success story and a beautiful person that truly has Smiled Through it All!

Archer Casey Senior Photographer Archer

Photography Kansas City, Mo

Andre K. Cavitt (Friend): To all concerned, my
name is Andre but to Ms. Pam, I'm better known as Dray. Pam and I met some time ago. I want to say it was in 2006 but it was around that time period. Once we met in person, immediately she and I hit it off. It could be because of both our easy going and carefree natures. At this time, Pam was living in Topeka, Ks and I was living in Manhattan, Ks. I did make it a point to visit Pam when I found myself in Topeka. In case you are not aware of these cities, these cities are about 50 miles from one another. During our friendship, I have had the opportunity to meet her family and friends. I guess you can say that when I

visit Pam when she returns to Topeka, I'm like one of the family. It's no big deal that I'm there. Pam has gone through some obstacles, but she continues to keep a positive attitude. I'm happy that you are a part of my life and I'm excited about this new chapter in your life. Know that you are blessed and highly favored. I look forward to reading your book.

Your friend always. Andre K.

Shirley Harmon (Aunt): My name is Shirley Harmon. I am writing on behalf of Pamela Harmon-Porter. Pam is my niece through marriage to her uncle. Pam is a very energetic and outgoing person who knows what she wants out of life. Pam is the mother of two sons, Marlon and Corebin whom she cares for deeply. Pam loves being with her sibling family and relatives and always staying connected with them. She tries to visit family when she can. I remember just a few years ago, she was told at the last minute that one of her uncles was having an 80th birthday celebration the next day in Mississippi. She made it a point to travel to Mississippi from Atlanta the very next day to be at the celebration. Pam loves her family. Whenever I travel going through the Atlanta area, I always notify her that I'm passing through. Pam goes out her way to makes sure she visits with me during my stay. She loves traveling to various places. She's a beautiful person once you get to know her. I'm proud to be her aunt and a member of the family.

Derrick Nesby (Friend): My name is Derrick Nesby, Pam Porter is my ex-girlfriend. Pam is a loving, beautiful, caring person and even though we are not together. She is still in my life as a good friend.

Rainie Hernanandez-Harmon (Niece): My Aunt Pam is probably one of the strongest and most positive people in my life. Between bad situations and bad people, she's always come out on top. Although she would claim to be a shy person, I believe her to be one of the most social and relatable people I've grown to know. Making her an extremely easy person to be able to talk to. I know that if I were to ever need anything I would be able to count on her to be present. I wish her nothing but the best from this life.

J. Eric Armstrong (Friend): Pamela Porter is a determined, hardworking and reliable person that I am lucky enough to call friend for the past 20 years. A devoted and loving single mom, who has seen life's ups and downs facing them head on. Brave enough to adapt to change and smart enough to overcome obstacles. I wish more people were as kind, loving and devoted. I'll always be your greatest supporter.

Eric

Marcus Hawkins (Friend): We have known each other since before I went to Iraq and during that time we have had plenty of good moments of sharing our ups and downs. I still consider you as my friend even though we don't conversate like we use to back in the day. Life has taken us into different directions but the friendship still remains.

Glossary

What is my personality type?

Can you guess my personality type? Are you a little confused as to what it really is – A Cancer woman's personality type is chirpy, somber or distant? She is all of these and still, she is none of these. Even more confused? This personality type has mood swings every now and then and these are only a few of her mood swings. However, her basic personality traits remain the same. She is very sensitive, emotional, kind and caring. Now's the catch! Most of her traits will be hidden behind a shell of indifference and aloofness, breaking which will require quite a lot of effort. You will have to gently coerce this girl to get out of her shell and come into the big bad world. When in love, she will be tender, womanly, timid and modest. She dislikes criticisms, can't stand rejection and gets deeply hurt by harsh words. Too much aggressiveness on your part may make her a little hesitant. She loves her mother, so you better learn to love as well as respect her too. This woman will never make the first moves in a relationship; she only knows how to move backwards or sideways. This is because of two reasons, her shyness and her fear of being rejected. This female has some secrets and she won't like you prying around her personal diary. She is very insecure and will need your constant reassurance. It doesn't matter if she is the current 'Miss Universe' or has men drooling over her all the time, it is your attention and appreciation she would be the most concerned about. You will have to learn to live with this woman's mood swings, which is not so difficult since she is so good in every other way. She is extremely loyal and will keep you happy with her

warm and rich humor. Once she is committed to you,

she will remain yours forever and ever. Adultery is

not one of her traits. With this woman, you will

always have to be careful with words. She is very

sentimental and can get hurt very easily. Then, she

can cry like a 2-year old baby and you will be expected

to console her and wipe her tears. This female is a

great cook and makes better food than a 5-star hotel

chef. She is quite careful with money as well. Neither

will she be stingy, nor totally extravagant. She has a

habit of saving everything that is usable, be it money,

old buttons or empty jars. She also saves things that

have a sentimental value attached to them, like the

sweater grandmother knitted on her fifth birthday.

This female fiercely guards what is hers and that

includes you too! However, she is not too possessive

or jealous. But, she does not like sharing her love too. She is one of those people who do not crib about bad luck. She will get depressed and may shed a few tears alone, but she will be patient and wait for the time to change again, this time in her favor. Almost all of the women with this personality type have the desire of being pampered like a child, especially when they feel low. Don't forget to pay your girl extra attention when she is depressed, otherwise she may retreat deeper into her shell and then, it will be very difficult to bring her back to her normal self. She will want to be told time and again that she is still desirable and you still need her. However, she is not weak and is completely capable of looking after herself. In fact, she is one of those who sacrifice all that they have for their loved ones. She just needs some spoiling after every few days. This woman may be fragile as far as

her feelings are concerned, but when you need her,
she will be as strong as the 'Rock of Gibraltar'. She
will also be very protective of her children and make
them feel completely secure. Kids will be the center
of her universe and she will pamper them with her
love, affection and care. The children will also be very
close to her and no matter how much far they go
from home, they will come back to her and she will
know this. This female always needs you, but she will
never get too aggressive. She knows that you may
leave for a while, to follow your dreams, but in the
end, she is the one you will come back to. Then, you
will find her as charming as before, waiting for you
with freshly baked bread and hot soup. She will feed
you, listen to your worries and make you smile again!
http://www.iloveindia.com

Domestic violence

What is Domestic Violence?

Domestic Violence is a violent confrontation between family or household members involving physical harm, sexual assault, or fear of physical harm. Family or household members include spouses / former spouses, those in (or formerly in) a dating relationship, adults related by blood or marriage, and those who have a biological or legal parent-child relationship. The batterer uses acts of violence and a series of behaviors, including intimidation, threats, psychological abuse, and isolation to coerce and to control the other person. The violence may not happen often, but may remain a hidden and constant terrorizing factor. Domestic violence is not only physical and sexual violence but also psychological. Psychological violence means intense and repetitive degradation, creating isolation, and controlling the actions or behaviors of the spouse through intimidation or manipulation to the detriment of the individual. Domestic violence destroys the home. No one deserves to be abused. The responsibility for the violence belongs to the abuser. It is not the victim's fault!

Symptoms of Abuse:

Misuse of Power and Control Abuse in a relationship is any act used to gain power and control over another person. Women who are abused physically are often isolated. Their partners tend to control their lives to a great extent as well as verbally degrade them.

Physical and Sexual Abuse:

Hair pulling, biting, shaking, pushing, pinching, choking, kicking, confinement, slapping, hitting, punching, using weapons, forced intercourse, unwanted sexual touching in public or in private and depriving her of food or sleep.

Emotional Abuse:

Insulting him/her in public or in private. Putting down her friends and family. Making her feel bad about herself. Calling her names Making her think she's crazy. Playing mind games. Humiliating her Making her feel guilty. Using Male Privilege; acting like "Master of the Castle". Treating her like a servant. Making all the big decisions. Being the one to define men's and women's roles.

Economic Abuse:

Preventing her from getting or keeping a job. Making

her ask for money. Giving her an allowance. Taking

her money. Not letting her know about or have access

to family income. Not allowing her a voice in

important financial decisions. Demanding exclusive

control over household finances. Using coercion and

threats. Making or carrying out threats to do

something to hurt her Threatening to leave her, or to

commit suicide. Threatening to report her to welfare.

Making her drop charges Making her do illegal things.

Using intimidation. Making her afraid by using looks,

gestures, or actions. Throwing or smashing things.

Destroying property. Abusing pets. Dangerous

driving. Displaying weapons. Using children. Making

her feel guilty about the children. Using the children

to relay messages. Using visitation to harass her. Threatening to take the children away.

Isolation:

Controlling what she does, who she sees, what she reads, & where she goes. Limiting her outside involvement. Refusing to let her learn to drive, go to school, or get a job. Not allowing her to freely use the car or the telephone.

Jealousy and blame to justify actions:

Minimizing, Denying, Blaming Making light of the abuse and not taking her concerns about it seriously. Checking up on where she's been or who she's talked to. Accusing her of infidelity. Saying the abuse didn't happen. Shifting responsibility for abusive behavior. Saying she caused it. Why Get Help? The danger is real.

Are you a Victim of Domestic Violence?

1. Is your partner threatening or violent towards you or the children?

2. Do you find yourself making excuses or minimizing your partner's behavior?

3. Do you feel completely controlled by your partner?

4. Do you feel helpless, trapped, alone, and isolated?

5. Do you blame yourself for the violence?

6. Does your partner blame you and tell you that you are the cause of all his problems?

7. Do you blame the violence on stress, on drugs/alcohol, or a bad childhood?

8. Does your partner constantly accuse you of having affairs when he can't account for 100% of your time? Does he tell you jealousy is a sign of love?

9. Do you fear going home?

10. Are you limited in your freedom like a child? (Go to the store and come straight home. It should take you 15 minutes.)

11. Do you find yourself lying to hide your partner's real behavior (for example, saying you fell down the stairs when actually you were pushed)?

12. Are you embarrassed or humiliated by your partner in an effort to control your behavior, especially in public?

13. Does your partner abandon you, leave you places, or lock you out?

14. Does your partner hide your keys, mail, or other important papers? This info comes from http://www.clarkprosecutor.org/html/domviol/what.htm 47

What can I do?

If you are controlling or have a controlling partner, don't ignore these behaviors. They are not the result of stress, anger, drugs or alcohol. They are learned behaviors that one person uses to dominate, intimidate and manipulate. They are destructive and dangerous. If the abuse continues without outside help, the abusing partner may risk being arrested, going to jail, or losing the relationship. Domestic violence hurts all family members. When a person is abusive he or she eventually loses the trust and respect of his or her partner. Abused partners are afraid to communicate their feelings and needs. Everyone has the right to feel safe in a relationship. With help, people who are abusive can learn to be non-violent. Learn the Warning Signs. Disagreements

develop from time to time in relationships.
Domestic violence is not a disagreement. It is a
whole pattern of behaviors used by one partner to
establish and maintain power and control over
the other. These behaviors can become more
frequent and intense over time. The abusive
person is responsible for these behaviors. That
person is the only one who can change them.
Don't wait until you and the ones you love get
hurt. You Are Not Alone. Consider getting some
help. Talk with friends about your situation.

Alzheimer

What is Alzheimer? A degenerative brain disease of unknown cause that is the most common form of dementia, that usually starts in late middle age or in old age, that results in progressive memory loss, impaired thinking, disorientation, and changes in personality and mood, and that is marked histologically by the degeneration of brain neurons especially in the cerebral cortex and by the presence of neurofibrillary tangles and plaques containing beta-amyloid —called also Alzheimer's

http://www.merriamwebster.com/dictionary/Alzheimer's

Alopecia

What is alopecia areata? Alopecia areata is a type of hair loss that occurs when your immune system mistakenly attacks hair follicles, which is where hair growth begins. The damage to the follicle is usually not permanent. Experts do not know why the immune system attacks the follicles. Alopecia areata is most common in people younger than 20, but children and adults of any age may be affected. Women and men are affected equally. What happens in alopecia areata? Alopecia areata usually begins when clumps of hair fall out, resulting in totally smooth, round hairless patches on the scalp. In some cases, the hair may become thinner without noticeable patches of baldness, or it may grow and break off, leaving short stubs (called "exclamation point" hair).

171

In rare cases, complete loss of scalp hair and body hair occurs. The hair loss often comes and goes-hair will grow back over several months in one area but will fall out in another area. When alopecia areata results in patches of hair loss, the hair usually grows back in a few months. Although the new hair is usually the same color and texture as the rest of the hair, it sometimes is fine and white. About 10% of people with this condition may never regrow hair.

You are more likely to have permanent hair loss if you:

• Have a family history of the condition.

• Have the condition at a young age (before puberty) or   for longer than 1 year.

• Have another autoimmune disease.

• Are prone to allergies (atopy).

• Have extensive hair loss.

• Have abnormal color, shape, texture, or thickness of the fingernails or toenails.

Because hair is an important part of appearance, hair loss can result in feeling unattractive. In some people with alopecia areata, the fingernails and toenails become pitted-they look as if a pin had made many tiny dents in them. They may also look like sandpaper. Alopecia areata cannot be "cured" but it can be treated. Most people who have one episode will have more episodes of hair loss.

webmd.com

www.ingramcontent.com/pod-product-compliance
Lightning Source LLC
Chambersburg PA
CBHW041214030426
42336CB00023B/3342